MW00940697

Daily Success
THE BOOK SERIES

WAYS TO
ROCK YOUR
WORLD

Everyday Activities for Success Every Day

Other Books by Dayna Steele

Rock to the Top:
What I Learned about Success from
the World's Greatest Rock Stars

Other Works by Bill Hinds

Tank McNamara
Buzz Beamer

WAYS TO ROCK YOUR WORLD

Everyday Activities for Success Every Day

Based on the popular FastCompany.com Expert Perspective blog post
5 Things To Do Every Day For Success

DAYNA STEELE

DAILY SUCCESS PUBLISHING
USA

101 Ways to Rock Your World
Everyday Activities for Success Every Day

Daily Success Publishing books may be ordered
through booksellers or by contacting:

books@yourdailysuccesstip.com
www.yourdailysuccesstip.com

Images @ Daily Success LLC
Author photos courtesy of Brett Chisholm
ISBN-13: 978-1519632319
ISBN-10: 1519632312

The only guarantee this book comes with is that if you want to be
successful, the author guarantees you will have to work for it.
The tips in this book are merely suggestions. However, you'll never
know if they work if you don't at least try them—every day.

To Charlie, Cris, Dack, and Nick,

I love you more every day.

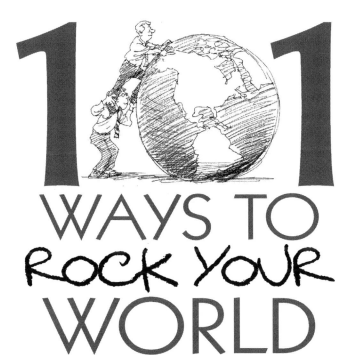

WAYS TO
ROCK YOUR
WORLD

Everyday Activities for Success Every Day

Success might mean, but is not limited to, a level of social status, achievement of an objective/goal, or the opposite of failure.

—Definition from Wikipedia

Contents

Foreword by Guy Kawasaki

Success requires relationships—business, marriage, parenting, friendship, and partnership. These are uncomplicated words that define our most complicated interactions.

Success also requires perseverance and immersion. There is a chasm when people try to disseminate a vision from "me" to "many." It is easy to engage in your personal vision. It is much more difficult to convince others to share that vision.

Dayna Steele has simple and pure answers for these issues. She has created a straightforward yet very achievable list of tips to get you started on the path to success.

Her success is neither a surprise nor the result of luck.

Dayna starts with a mantra—not a business plan—that is only three words long: "Create rock stars."

Do you want to be a rock star? If so, read this book.

Guy Kawasaki is the author of eleven books, including What the Plus!, Reality Check, The Art of the

Start, Rules for Revolutionaries, How to Drive Your Competition Crazy, Selling the Dream, *and* The Macintosh Way. *He is also the cofounder of Alltop.com, an "online magazine rack" of popular topics on the web, and a founding partner at Garage Technology Ventures. Previously, he was the chief evangelist of Apple. Kawasaki has a BA from Stanford University and an MBA from UCLA, as well as an honorary doctorate from Babson College.*

Acknowledgments

It's always important to remember to thank people who help you along the way with anything (see tip #52). With that said, let me first start by saying thank you for buying and reading my first book, *Rock to the Top: What I Learned about Success from the World's Greatest Rock Stars*. You are the rock star who inspires me to keep writing, posting, blogging, speaking, teaching, and preaching about success.

To Wilene Dunn, who read the first book and then had the courage to call me and say, "I want to meet you, and I am going to work for you someday." She has become an amazing partner in my speech business, encouraging me to keep writing and keep speaking around the globe spreading the rock-star principles of success.

To FastCompany.com for asking me to become a regular blogger for their "Expert Leaders" (now Expert Perspective) series and Judy Haveson who suggested I write posts for this website. My FastCompany.com blog post "5 Things to Do Every Day for Success" went viral worldwide and inspired this book thanks to the efforts of Erin Collier, Kevin Ohannessian, and the entire FastCompany.com crew. Thanks for inviting me to the party.

To Steeleworkers everywhere for commenting and making suggestions on my blogs and social media on a regular basis, as well as joining me in person at speeches and appearances, to share your ideas and success stories. You rock!

To the many speakers bureaus and agents who represent my presentations around the world, thank you for allowing me to spread the concepts of reachable success to my Steeleworkers worldwide. Also, thank you for the groceries, the roof over my head, the utilities, and gas money, as well as my kids' college funds.

To Susan Neuhalfen and Linda Lee for their friendship and their red editing pens.

To Lisa Waymire Hinds for being my best friend in elementary school and for marrying Bill Hinds, so I could eventually meet him and have a great illustrator for this book.

To Mom and Dad, who gave me a love of success and the work ethic that goes along with it, as well as the pride in knowing you've done a good job *and* you've done the right thing.

To Charlie, Cris, Dack, and Nick—the loves of my life.

Everyday is a single word and is an adjective, used in front of a noun to describe something as normal or commonplace.

Every day is an adjective plus a noun, and it means each day.

Your Daily List

The Merriam-Webster dictionary defines *success* as "a favorable or desired outcome; also, the attainment of wealth, favor, or eminence."

In March 2011, I wrote a simple blog post for FastCompany.com as a part of their "Expert Leaders" (now Expert Perspective) blog series. "5 Things to Do Every Day for Success" was inspired by several conversations with friends, family members, and audience participants after my speech presentations about how to be successful. Most of those conversations started with this question: "You seem to be doing well. How do you do it?"

If you have enough of those conversations, you start to realize "success" is no different from the elusive Holy Grail: many want it but don't know where to find it or how to achieve it—or, more importantly, where to start.

The beginning of any success story is to set a strong foundation and create a "personal brand" for you. You create or start both by habit, consistency, reliability, and creativity—every day.

I wrote the FastCompany.com post as a simple list of how to get started on everyday success with these simple everyday activities:

- Wake up early.
- Review the news.
- Send something to someone who can give you money for your product or service.
- Contact an old acquaintance you have not spoken with in a while.
- Write a handwritten note to someone.

Then the strangest, most wonderful thing happened with the original blog post. It struck a chord with people around the world and started to go "viral" in May 2011, then again all summer and fall of that year, and as of this writing, it remains in the top ten most-read posts for the FastCompany.com "Expert Leaders" (now Expert Perspective) blog series. It appears people just need a starting point to reach their own success in terms they can understand and can start with immediately. It was that simple.

Success can mean many things to many people, but ultimately, success is defined as what makes you happy and satisfied with your own life. Whether you want to be Steve Jobs, Warren Buffett, or Bill Gates, or just pay your bills and have time to play, the suggestions in this book will help you set a foundation for success each and every day in whatever you do.

There will be the naysayers who say this list is too simple, that these are things you should have learned from your parents or early on in your career. (See what I have to say about this in #83.) There will be those who say there is no way you can do all 101 suggestions in this book every day. Then there will be the others who will attempt to do all 101 suggestions in this book every day until they drive themselves, and everyone around them, crazy.

What I suggest is that you read the book and start to incorporate the suggestions into your daily routine until they become habit. Once you do so, you will not need the list anymore. You will be too busy being successful to worry about anything else. Simply put, you must be brilliant at the basics in order to succeed at the next level.

Most importantly, just as beauty is in the eye of the beholder, remember that success can only be defined by you.

It is amazing how many people are too busy to succeed.

—Dave Ramsey

Five Things to Do Every Day for Success

Originally posted on FastCompany.com

1.   Wake up early.*

For the next week, get up half an hour earlier than you normally do ... *and get going!* If you get a few more things done, then get up even earlier the next week. Early in the morning is a great time to get work done because most of your associates have not started e-mailing, tweeting, calling, texting, or posting yet.

*This, by the way, is the number one activity or tip others want to argue with me about. So let me clarify. Be up well before the people who give you money (customers, clients, fans) and before your competition. If your fans (again, customers and clients) work and give you money during the day, then get up early in the morning. If they give you money at night, well, lucky you, you get to sleep in.

The ability to convert ideas to things is the secret to outward success.

—Henry Ward Beecher

2.   Pay attention to the news.

Read the headlines and watch the news. You will not only know what is going on in the world, but will also be the first to recognize opportunities for you and your business (if you followed #1) long before the competition has even had their first cup of coffee.

3. Get in touch with someone you have not talked to in a while.

Touch base with old friends or associates you have not talked to in ages. Ask how they are, what they are working on, and ask or suggest how you might help. You will make their day. You will have also added another person to your current network of people you know. Remember the old show business saying: "It's not what you know but who you know."

Always bear in mind that your own resolution to suc-ceed is more important than any one thing.

—Abraham Lincoln

4. Send something to someone who can give you money.

Send something to one person who can hire you or buy your product at some point in the future. Maybe it is something you promised to follow up with, a quick e-mail with a link to something relevant, or a "Hey, just checking in to see how things are going" e-mail. It could also be a birthday card, an invoice, a gift, a lead, a client, an interesting link—anything. This will keep you top-of-mind with this person, and that is a good thing when he or she gets in the mood to spend some money.

5. Write a handwritten note to someone.

Seriously. It is a lost art and makes quite an impression. There is always someone you can send a note to, whether it is a thank-you note, a birthday card, or just a "hello" note. The fact it is handwritten makes a powerful impact on the receiver, and it also stands out in the mound of junk mail we receive weekly. I promise a handwritten note will not go unnoticed.

The Other Ninety-Six

Some people succeed because they are destined to, but most people succeed because they are determined to.

—Unknown

6.   Stretch.

Have you ever watched cats or dogs get up from their naps? They take a nice long stretch and then bound off. Enough said.

7. Eat a good breakfast.

Your mother was right: always start the day with a good breakfast, including plenty of protein. If you start the day with sugary foods or no food, your blood-sugar levels will play havoc with your energy and ability to concentrate and focus.

8.   Brush your teeth.

Really? You are a grown adult, and I should not have to tell you this. Do this every morning, every night, and every chance in between. When is the last time you chose to do business with someone with missing teeth or nasty breath?

9. Take a shower to start your day.

You will clean off any perspiration and dead skin cells from your night's sleep and be more invigorated and confident for social situations. Plus, the shower is a great place for coming up with ideas or belting out your favorite song.

10. Dress for the job you want.

The way you dress is a big part of your personal brand. Look at the people who are where you want to be—how are they dressed? It is okay to create your own style, but remember, the way you are dressed is all a part of the first impression you make on people. And first impressions are hard to change.

11. Have a plan for the day.

Each morning, after you have had a chance to look at your calendar, e-mail, and social media sites, make a list—in order of priority and times—of what needs to be accomplished that day and where you need to be at what time. Also note when you need to leave to get where you are going on time (or even a little early). Handwritten or digital, you can keep up with what has to be done so you will not forget anything. It is a good feeling to delete or cross out each item as you proceed. Also, if you do not get it all done, you know what is left to do and can add that to tomorrow's list.

12. Move profit-generating activities earlier in the day.

First of all, if you do not do it, someone else will. Be the first to get a jump on the project or client. Then you have the rest of the day to make it work and be the best.

Action is the foundational key to all success.
—Pablo Picasso

13. Pick one thing you want to accomplish each day.

Things happen, events change, people cancel. Realize your plan for the day will be fluid and you will have to make changes. Pick the one thing that—no matter what happens—you will get done today. Then git'er done!

14. Drink water.

Water is good for you. Water helps maintain a healthy weight, gives you healthy-looking skin, flushes toxins from your body, and even cushions your joints and muscles. By the way, did you know you could use a soft drink to take stuck bugs off a car windshield or remove battery acid from a car battery? Think about that the next time you want a soda. Have a glass of water instead.

15. Work harder than anyone else.

When asked to what he attributed his success, my longtime agent, Troy Blakely, without hesitation gave me this tip. Everybody wants to be a rock star. Not everybody wants to do the work it takes to be a rock star. Think about the successful people you know— they are pretty darned busy, aren't they?

16. Take responsibility for your own actions.

You have no one to blame but yourself. Figure out what went wrong and why. Learn from it and move on. Then, do not do it again.

17. Verbalize what you want or need to another person.

Only your mother can read your mind. Always ask for what you need. Speak up. Most people are happy to help. If they are not, move on. No drama. Move forward. Then ask someone else.

Dream up the kind of world you want to live in. Dream out loud.

—Bono

18. Act like you cannot fail.

What would you do if you knew you could not fail? Do it. If you do fail? Read on.

19. Learn from the mistake if you do fail.

There is a lesson to learn in every mistake and in every failure. The most successful people in the world fail all the time. It is because they take chances and look for new things to try. Some will work and some will not, but you will never know if you do not try. Steve Jobs had a few misses. He did okay.

I have never failed; I have only found ten thousand ways not to make a lightbulb.

—Thomas Edison

20. Take a walk.

You would be surprised how many times you have the opportunity to walk and you just ignore that opportunity. Do not take the closest parking space; take the one at the back of the parking lot. Go around the building to another door. Walk to a restaurant for that business lunch. Get your heart and your feet moving; your brain will follow.

You can bitch, or you can do something to change your situation. I prefer the latter.

—Peter Shankman

21. Eat healthy foods.

There is really not a lot to say here. You know what is healthy and what is not. Fat, fried, sugar, soft drinks—not good. Lean meat, vegetables, fruits, water—good. Former Arkansas governor Mike Huckabee once told me in an interview, "If it comes through a window, it's probably not good for you."

22. Talk to a stranger.

You are no longer five. It is okay to talk to strangers. In fact, you will find that most people have a great story if you just say hello, introduce yourself, and talk to them. Cabdrivers, someone in an elevator or in line at the theater—that stranger could be your next best friend or biggest client. You will never know unless you speak to a stranger.

A candle loses nothing when it lights another candle.
—Thomas Jefferson

23. Make someone else laugh or smile.

It is a great feeling to make another person smile or laugh. When you feel good, you will have more energy and will be more creative. What goes around, comes around.

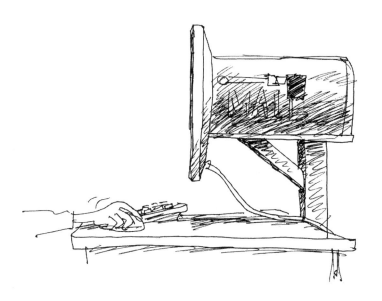

24. Check e-mail smartly.

It is very easy to start checking e-mails and, all of a sudden, find yourself off task for an hour. Or two. Or three. Figure out what schedule works best for you so you still can keep your clients and customers happy—it may be every five minutes or a couple of times a day. First of all, acknowledge you received an e-mail and *not* with an autoresponder. If you do not respond quickly, especially to those who can give you money, chances are whoever it is will move on to the next person on his or her list. Create a file system within your e-mail program where you can prioritize everything you receive and need to react to. As for the crap—delete it, unsubscribe from it, create a junk-mail protocol, whatever it takes to keep it to a minimum so you can concentrate on the e-mails that will translate into success. Clean out the noise and be able to re-spond immediately to the good stuff.

25. Learn the name of someone you are always around.

There is a lady who sweeps the floors at our local post office. Her name is Martha. As far as I can tell, I'm the only one who has ever bothered to ask her name. I greet her each morning by name. She smiles. I smile. Everyone is important enough that others should know his or her name. When you take that first step, you never know—you may be adding a very important person to your network of success. Even better, maybe a good friend. It all starts with the name.

To climb steep hills requires a slow pace at first.

—William Shakespeare

26. Drive the speed limit.

People who drive the speed limit are more likely to live longer lives and have lower insurance rates. It is really difficult to be successful when you are dead.

27. Research someone you are meeting with or talking to today.

Whether it is a meeting with a client, a job interview, a conference call, or just a casual lunch, do a simple web search beforehand. There is no excuse anymore to not know something about that person prior to the meeting. Check his or her social media as well; it will always give you the upper hand to walk into a meeting with that knowledge.

28. Think positive.

Negativity breeds so many bad things—stress, lack of companionship, missed opportunities, and the list goes on. It takes a lot less energy to be positive— energy you can be using for something great, like your successful life.

They can because they think they can.

—Virgil

29. Always try to say yes.*

When you say yes to invitations, requests, opportunities, meetings—anything you can—you meet all kinds of new people and experience amazing new adventures. When you say no all the time, people stop asking. There is always a way to say yes.

*The amazing Guy Kawasaki says the same thing. I am so appreciative that he said yes to the foreword for this book!

30. Introduce two people who can help each other.

Whether it is getting clients together or fixing up friends on a date, put people together and stand back and watch. Your network will grow when you help others grow their network.

No man becomes rich unless he enriches others.
—Andrew Carnegie

31. Return e-mails and phone calls.

Always respond to e-mails and phone calls within 48 hours—even if it is just to say, "I am swamped and will get back with you as soon as I can." If you give out your number or e-mail, then do not act put out when someone contacts you.

32. Examine a coincidence.

I am a firm believer that things happen for a reason; there are no coincidences. Take a moment to look at the situation and see if you can find the opportunity in what just happened.

33. Try to do something differently.

Change something in your routine today: find a new way to work, a new way to wear your hair, a different food, a different chair, or a different way of dressing. It may or may not be better than what you were doing, but it will keep you interesting and sharp.

The secret of success is to know something nobody else knows.

—Aristotle Onassis

To be successful, you have to have your heart in your business, and your business in your heart.

—Thomas Watson Sr.

34. Do your homework.

Homework equals preparation. Preparation equals confidence. A simple Internet search will, more likely than not, bring up a wealth of information on anything you need to know. Never go into any meeting or situation blind. Always know what you are going into and use the resources we all have (but few take the time) to use.

35. Read an inspirational quote out loud.

It is like having an imaginary friend give you a pep talk. In the shower, on your walk, as you are getting ready for the day, find a quote at random or from someone you admire and read it out loud.

36. Be brief, to the point, and relevant.

You and I are inundated with so many messages from so many different sources each day that much of it is lost in the noise. You will make your message stand out when you are brief, to the point, and relevant in all that you write, including e-mails, texts, posts, and blogs, as well as in what you say.

Quality is more important than quantity. One home run is much better than two doubles.

—Steve Jobs

37. Do something to help someone else be successful.

You get what you give—many times over. This is actually the key to successful networking, as opposed to passing out business cards. It can be as simple as e-mailing an informative link or passing on a client lead. Think of it as "business karma."

38. Pretend you are your customer and review the experience.

From top to bottom, from beginning to end, step into your customer's shoes and see what the experience is really like. Oh boy, are you in for surprises.

Bonus tip: When a customer calls or e-mails to ask a question, you probably have ten more customers who did not bother to ask and went elsewhere. Always figure out what you can do to keep another customer from having to ask that same question.

The main thing is to care. Care very hard, even if it is only a game you are playing.
                                              —Billie Jean King

39. Ask someone you trust to step into your shoes.

It is good to get another perspective on what you do, your personal brand, or your product or service. Ask him or her what he or she would do differently if he or she were you. Then act on those suggestions and see what happens. Good or bad, you'll learn from it.

Success is falling down nine times and getting up ten.

—Jon Bon Jovi

40. Ask for a referral or introduction.

Just when you think you know everything there is to know about someone, you find out yet one more thing. You never really know whom someone is connected to or what he or she is capable of doing for you if you do not ask. Make sure people in your network know what you want or need or hope to do someday. And whom you need to meet.

Life is too short to have anything but delusional notions about yourself.

—Gene Simmons

41. Seize every opportunity to network.

Networking is not just something you do at business functions. Anytime two or more people are gathered together, anywhere, that is networking. It could be at a social gathering, waiting at the train station, or even at your child's school function. Talk to people, introduce yourself, ask about them, and listen to their answers. The more people you get to know, the larger and more successful your network becomes.

As good as I am, I'm nothing without my band.
—Steven Tyler

42. Do something for a charity organization.

On any given day, there are thousands of charitable organizations that could use your help. It could be in the form of a donation, your time, or just making your network aware of an organization or event. Every little bit helps.

43. Actually pick up the phone and call someone.

We are humans. We were built to actually talk to each other occasionally. So many people do not bother to call anymore that, if you do, you will stand out from the crowd. Novel, I know, but pick up the phone and give it a try.

Success comes in cans, failure in can'ts.

—Unknown

44. Have a firm handshake.

Nothing leaves a lasting impression like a cold, clammy, weak handshake or a bone-crushing squeeze. Learn to shake hands so that you convey confidence and respect, not wussiness or domination. Practice on friends and ask how your handshake really is perceived. Old-fashioned but telling.

There are only two rules for being successful. One, figure out exactly what you want to do, and two, do it.

—Mario Cuomo

45. Read a magazine or visit a website on a subject you know nothing about or do not even like.

When you do this, not only do you become that much more interesting and informed, but you will also discover something new or maybe even find a new solution to an old problem.

46. Do not burn bridges.

Go out of your way to *not* alienate a friend, potential customer, ally, or stranger. In other words, be nice. You never know when you may need or run into that person again. This includes, but is not limited to, the line at the post office, the airline counter, the driver's license office, and the grocery store.

Success is a lousy teacher. It seduces smart people into thinking they can't lose.

—Bill Gates

47. Read or watch something that motivates or inspires you.

Always stay inspired—it is what keeps us going. Fortunately, we all have friends who keep us supplied with a wealth of this type of material on Facebook and YouTube. Watch one of the videos or read one of the stories. If it moved your friend, it will probably move you and inspire you to keep going.

Flaming enthusiasm, backed up by horse sense and persistence, is the quality that most frequently makes for success.

—Dale Carnegie

48. Give someone a gift for no reason.

When is the last time you walked into the office with a box of cupcakes for no reason other than to give everyone cupcakes? Do this for employees, clients, loved ones, even the crew at a place where you shop. You would be amazed at the power of a cupcake or a cookie or anything that is nice and unexpected.

49. Be curious.

When you are curious, you learn. When you learn, you are more successful. When you are more successful, you are happy. That is what I like about toddlers—they skip that middle part altogether and go straight from curious to happy. If you hear something you do not understand, look it up. If you see something you have never seen before, ask questions, pick it up, turn it over. Be a wide-eyed toddler sometimes.

50. Keep a diary or write a blog.

Writing on a daily basis keeps the creative juices flow-ing, gives you an outlet, and gives other people some-thing interesting (hopefully) to read if you post it. It is also a good thing to go back and read someday to see where you were at a certain point in your life. And it helps with your spelling and grammar capabilities—always a good thing.

51. Don't smoke.

Smoking kills people. You do not stand in front of a moving car, do you?

You must do the thing you think you cannot do.
                                                —Eleanor Roosevelt

52. Say thank you.

To everyone. For everything. Period.

Don't confuse fame with success. Madonna has one;
Helen Keller has the other.

—Erma Bombeck

53.   Believe in yourself.

The very first step to success in anything is believing you can do it. If you do not believe, how do you expect others to believe in you?

If you don't quit, and don't cheat, and don't run home when trouble arrives, you can only win.
—Shelley Long

54. Make a decision.

Access the facts, check your gut, and make a decision. The longer you wait, the better chance you have of someone else making the decision for you. Odds are, you will not like it.

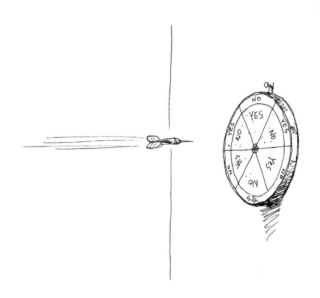

55. Spend only what you have.

Credit cards were originally created for convenience, not for you to get what you want when you want it just because you want it. Pay cash for things or use your debit card. If you must use a credit card, maybe for business, pay it in full at the end of each monthly cycle—if not sooner.

56. Pet an animal.

Study after study has shown that when we pet a dog or cat, depending on preference, our blood pressure drops. It is almost impossible to stay in a bad mood when those big eyes look at you so adoringly. Some people get this warm, fuzzy feeling from a snake or other reptile. Hmm. To each his own.

57. Back up your files in a safe place.

At one point in my life, I had Academy Award-winning actor Clint Eastwood's private office number and a back line to the White House. I do not have either now because I never backed anything up. When my early version of the PDA crashed, I lost everything. Now, it is easy to back up your data. Do it. You will never be sorry you did. Go ahead, punk, make my day.

When I thought I couldn't go on, I forced myself to keep going. My success is based on persistence, not luck.

—Estee Lauder

58. Finish something you started.

Ahhh, procrastination, my old friend. (Come to think of it, that is not a very good friend to have at all.) The longer you put something off, the greater the chance you take of someone else doing it and taking off with your success.

59. Speak in front of a group.

Standing up in front of people and speaking is probably one of the biggest fears many have. Think of it
this way: it is like riding a bike. It is not easy at first and
sometimes you do crash, but after a while, if you keep
doing it, you get pretty good at it. Same thing.

60. Add at least one new entry to your network.

You meet so many people throughout a normal day. You should be adding at least one new person every day to your list of fans/customers/clients/friends. Gather contact information for your address book, follow others on Twitter, request a new Facebook friend—add to your network today.

61. Do not buy crap you do not need.

Drawers and closets are full of things we do not need. Open either one and look inside. How many things in there have you actually used in the last year? Part of being successful is having the money to do what you want or need to do when you want or need to do it. If you keep buying crap, you will be out of money when you need it the most.

62. Add to your emergency fund.

A few dollars every day adds up a lot faster than you would think. An emergency does not seem as bad when you have the means to take care of it.

63. Sync your computer, phone, and other electronics.

With today's technology, you should be able to access just about anything in your computer files on any device you have. Your desktop, laptop, tablet, and phone can all be synced to the same material. So when you meet potential clients and they need information, you can access it and get it to them immediately, while the competition has to wait to get back to the office. By the time they do, the client is yours. Added bonus—you then also have additional backups for your information, files, and contacts.

64. Get the most from your social media accounts.

Observe how your customers, clients, fans, or anyone who can give you money are using social media. Then interact with them on their terms, making it interesting, informative, or funny. Utilizing your social media platforms is a great way to brand you as the expert at something or as an interesting person people should know. If all you do is advertise, beg, berate, or play Farmville, chances are you're not looking to be successful—just irritating.

65. Keep your work area organized.

I did not say keep your work area neat; I said keep it organized. Make sure you can find the things you need when you need them. And do not organize for someone else unless they have asked you to help them organize their things. We all organize in different ways. I am a neat-freak organizer. Charlie the Wonder Husband is a messy organizer. We work in our own ways. I learned a long time ago not to straighten his office for him. He appreciates that, and it ain't bad for the marriage either!

Success is a science: if you have the conditions, you get the result.

—Oscar Wilde

66. Do something you have neglected.

We all have those things we put off day after day. I know what mine is, and you know what yours is. So just do it and get it over with. If it is something big, at least get it started or make some progress.

67. Do something that scares you.

Why not? What's the point of living if there is not a little adventure thrown in on a daily basis? Eventually I will do a tandem skydive—eventually.

68. Listen.

Stop and listen. Listen to the answer to a question you have just asked. Listen to the sounds around you. Listen to the other people talking at an event. Just listen. You will be amazed at what you hear.

69. Visualize what you want.

The human brain works in such mysterious ways. Sometimes just visualizing where you want to be or with the things you want to have is enough motivation to get the work done and make it happen. We are visual creatures—take advantage of that.

The ladder of success is best climbed by stepping on the rungs of opportunity.

—Ayn Rand

70. Learn how to do something new.

Go to YouTube or your favorite search engine and type in "how to ..." and see what comes up. Today I looked up "how to dougie." I do not do it very well, but I know how to do it now. Or, at the very least, I know what it means "to dougie."

71. Treat others the way you want to be treated.

A smile, a kind word, a please, a thank you—all go a long way to getting you what you need or want. Try doing the opposite of each, and you might as well be beating your head against a wall.

72. Talk to a mentor.

Even Bill Gates talks to Warren Buffet. Having someone around who has succeeded in his or her field and will share that knowledge is invaluable. Everyone should have a mentor. There is always someone smarter than you, and if you can get him or her to share that knowledge, how great is that? Just a thought: who is Warren Buffet's mentor?

73. Post an interesting article or blog.

First, it is nice to share. Second, it appears that you read, pay attention, are interesting, and keep up with things. Third, that makes people want to do business with you. Or, at the very least, be around you.

74.   Do not take out a loan.

Try saving your money until you can buy what you want
or need. It really can be done. You will be better for it
in the long run.

75. Throw something out that you have not used in a while.

A friend had this on her list of New Year's resolutions: "Throw out, give away, or recycle twenty-five things every day." I thought she was crazy until I tried it for a few days. Not only will you clean out all your stuff, but it also keeps you from buying more things when you realize just how much money you have wasted on things you really did not need. I bet you can find twenty-five things in one drawer alone!

Absorb what's useful, discard what's not, and add what's uniquely your own.

—Bruce Lee

76. Dare to be different.

Being a part of the pack is safe—and boring.

77. Eat a piece of chocolate.

This was suggested by several people after the original FastCompany blog post. I like these people.

78. Take a big breath and let it out slowly.

One of the things we do when we get stressed, concerned, or scared is hold our breath. This does absolutely no good for us and prevents us from thinking clearly. The next time you are concentrating strongly on a project at hand, remember to breathe.

Success or failure is caused more by mental attitude than by mental capacity.

—Sir Walter Scott

79. Review what is coming tomorrow before close of business today.

Check that plan you made at the beginning of the day. Did you miss anything? What's on the calendar for tomorrow? Review what is coming up so you can be prepared, and if something is missing or needs to be done, you have plenty of time to fix it and make it right.

Success is dependent on effort.

—Sophocles

80. Kiss your significant other like you did the first time.

Many studies have shown that people in monogamous relationships are healthier and live longer. Plus, this is just fun. No significant other? Tell your friends to fix you up. I went through a lot of bad blind dates—and kisses—to find Charlie the Wonder Husband.

81. Climb a flight of stairs.

Author and speaker Rory Vaden says that when you take the stairs, it becomes a metaphor for having the discipline to do the things we do not want to do but need to do. Taken literally, it will also give you a nice butt and is the exercise you thought you did not have time for today.

82. Listen to music.

Music opens up areas of your brain that you would not normally use while working. Added brainpower equals easier success over the long run.

That man is successful who has lived well, laughed often, and loved much; who has gained the respect of the intelligent men and the love of children; who has filled his niche and accomplished his task; who leaves the world better than he found it, whether by an improved poppy, a perfect poem, or a rescued soul; who never lacked appreciation of earth's beauty or failed to express it; who looked for the best in others and gave the best he had.

—Robert Louis Stevenson

83. Ignore the naysayers.

The more successful you become, the more negative people seem to target you and your actions. There will always be others who are jealous of your success and would love nothing more than to see you fail. Do not give them that satisfaction.

84. Smile.

It makes you look younger and successful. It has health benefits. It makes other people smile and puts them at ease. It really does make people think you have discovered the key to happiness, and they want to be around you to find out how you did it.

85. Laugh out loud.

A true, laugh-out-loud laugh relieves stress, elevates your mood, and usually stays with you the rest of the day. Search out humor in your day.

86. Do not give up.

Never take the first no or quit after the first failure. Keep going. Persistence does pay off. KLOL turned me down for a job three times. They hired me on the fourth try, and I was there for over fourteen years. It changed my life. With that said, read on ...

Try not to become a man of success, but rather try to become a man of value.

—Albert Einstein

87.   Follow your gut feelings.

You have amazing intuition, but like anything, if you do not use it, it gets rusty. Call it gut feeling, intuition, or crazy; it works. Pay attention to what your gut is saying. And if it is saying "it is time to move on"—then do so, and take the lessons learned onto your next endeavor.

88. Look people in the eye.

When you look someone in the eye, it conveys several messages: I care about what you are saying, I am paying attention to you, and I am telling you the truth and not hiding anything. These are all characteristics of someone people want to do business with.

89. Do not complain or speak badly of others.

No one cares. Really. I mean it. And it will make its way back to you.

90. Search your name online.

If someone is singing your praises or getting ready to trash your reputation, it will show up in an online search almost immediately. It is a good idea to set up an alert service so that this information comes straight to your e-mail on a regular basis. There are many free services, such as Google Alerts. You can set the service up with your name, your company name, your spouse, your kids, your product—anything you want to keep an eye on.

There is only one way to avoid criticism: do nothing, say nothing, and be nothing.

—Aristotle

91. Spend time with family and close friends.

This should be the most important group in your life. These are the people who most want to see you succeed, so be around them for that positive motivation as much as possible. If they do not want to see you succeed, you need new friends and family.

92. Share.

We were taught this early on, and many of us seem to have forgotten it somewhere along the way. Lunch, clients, information, leads, part of your chocolate—there are any number of things you can share during your day. Want to really have some fun? Try to share with strangers. It scares 'em to death at first, but then it usually breaks down a wall. Even if they decline your offer, I promise you have made them feel special.

93. Hug someone.

Nothing beats a hug. It makes everyone involved feel good.

94. Give yourself some downtime.

Sometimes you just need to stop and relax. Just a few moments where you do not answer calls and e-mails, you do not text and check Facebook, you do not socialize and engage. Just stop. Be still. Be quiet. Even if it is just for five minutes. Take some time out just for you and your peace of mind.

The toughest thing about success is that you've got to keep on being a success.

—Irving Berlin

95. Read a good book.

Obviously, you do not have time to read an entire book today, but at least read a few pages. If you commute using public transportation, that's a good time to read. Or before you go to sleep at night—keep a good book on your bedside table. It's good for your brain. Especially if you read books about successful people—you may find incredible inspiration from their story.

Formula for success: rise early, work hard, strike oil.
—J. Paul Getty

96.   Floss your teeth.

Studies have proven that people who floss their teeth live longer than those who do not. You can then use that extra time to become more successful.

97. Wash your face before you go to bed.

My mother used to tell me this when I was a teenager. Drove me crazy. I am glad she did, though; my skin still looks great at my age (do not even ask). Now I drive my kids crazy with the same thing. Make yourself get into the same habit. That is, the habit of washing your face, not driving your kids crazy.

Success is blocked by concentrating on it and planning for it ... Success is shy—it won't come out while you're watching.

—Tennessee Williams

98. Know when to quit for the day.

Done. The end. That is it. Whatever it is, it can wait until tomorrow morning (when you wake up early—see #1). Unless, of course, you are a brain surgeon—and I am assuming if you are, then you know when to quit.

99. Relax at the end of the day with a favorite beverage and go over your day with someone you are close to.

At the end of the day is a good time to go over your victories and your setbacks. Just talking about your day will inspire you to try again tomorrow. And it is nice to have someone to bounce things off at the end of the day—especially if they bring the wine.

100. Turn everything off at night.

Not only is it good for the environment and good for your electric bill, but it is also good for your health and you will get a better night's rest. No lights, sounds, bells, ringtones, alerts, tweets, whistles, television (even with the sound off), nada. Everything off.

101. Get a good night's rest.

Your body wants to sleep for a reason, so give it time to rest and reenergize for the next day. It is okay to sleep. It is okay to go to sleep early. Our bodies are amazing vessels if we just let them work the way they are supposed to.

For speaking and appearance information, media inquiries, and quantity book purchase discounts, contact info@daynasteele.com.

101 WAYS TO ROCK YOUR WORLD

Everyday Activities for Success Every Day

Based on the popular FastCompany.com Expert Perspective blog post
5 Things To Do Every Day For Success

DAYNA STEELE

Foreword by *Enchantment* author GUY KAWASAKI
Illustrated by BILL HINDS, cocreator of *Tank McNamara*

Your Biggest Fan

Success is many things to many people. To some, it may be a big mansion with an expensive car. To others, it may be a large company with a recognized name. To some, it is the ability to take time off and smell the roses. In the end, it all comes down to how *you* define success.

I used to think success was lots of money, that big house, a recognized name, and a Mercedes. Now I define success as the ability to do what I want, when I want, how I want, with whom I want, living life and conducting my businesses on my terms. All of my decisions, big or small, are now based on three criteria:

- Will it be fun?
- Will it give my family a great adventure?
- Will it put a smile on someone's face?

Being able to make decisions based on those three things brings me great joy and makes me feel successful. I live in an old house with well-worn furniture and, at this writing, drive a Toyota Prius with one hundred thousand miles on the odometer. I take time off several times a week to play golf, coach soccer, and hang out with family and friends. That would not be success to many others. It is to me, though, because it is what I want to do.

Overwhelmed by all my suggestions? No worries. You are probably already doing many of them and never really stopped to think about it. Another good thing is that many of these daily success actions can be combined. Sit still, visualize your success, and take a big breath. Smile and laugh out loud. Talk to a stranger and be curious. Dare to be different and do something that scares you. Take a walk and make a call to someone you have not talked to in a while. You get the idea.

To help you get started on this road to success, you'll find a checklist in the next section of this book. For the next couple of weeks, at the end of each day, go through the list and see how many you actually accomplished. You can also download the checklist off my website at www.daynasteele.com/rockstarsuccess and print out multiple copies.

Best of all, the more you do them, the more they become a part of your regular routine, and you will not even have to think about them anymore. You will just automatically do them, setting yourself up for success every day. After a while, you will not need the checklist or any success list. You will be too busy enjoying your successful life.

You can do this. I know you can because I'm your biggest fan.

Rock on!

Daily Success Checklist

1. □ Wake up early.
2. □ Pay attention to the news.
3. □ Get in touch with someone you have not talked to in a while.
4. □ Send something to someone who can give you money.
5. □ Write a handwritten note to someone.
6. □ Stretch.
7. □ Eat a good breakfast.
8. □ Brush your teeth.
9. □ Take a shower to start your day.
10. □ Dress for the job you want.
11. □ Have a plan for the day.
12. □ Move profit-generating activities earlier in the day.
13. □ Pick one thing you want to accomplish each day.
14. □ Drink water.
15. □ Work harder than anyone else.
16. □ Take responsibility for your own actions.
17. □ Verbalize what you want or need to another person.
18. □ Act like you cannot fail.
19. □ Learn from the mistake if you do fail.
20. □ Take a walk.
21. □ Eat healthy foods.

22. ☐ Talk to a stranger.
23. ☐ Make someone else laugh or smile.
24. ☐ Check e-mail smartly.
25. ☐ Learn the name of someone you are always around.
26. ☐ Drive the speed limit.
27. ☐ Research someone you are meeting with or talking to today.
28. ☐ Think positive.
29. ☐ Always try to say yes.
30. ☐ Introduce two people who can help each other.
31. ☐ Return e-mails and phone calls.
32. ☐ Examine a coincidence.
33. ☐ Try to do something differently.
34. ☐ Do your homework.
35. ☐ Read an inspirational quote out loud.
36. ☐ Be brief, to the point, and relevant.
37. ☐ Do something to help someone else be successful.
38. ☐ Pretend you are your customer and review the experience.
39. ☐ Ask someone you trust to step into your shoes.
40. ☐ Ask for a referral or introduction.
41. ☐ Seize every opportunity to network.
42. ☐ Do something for a charity organization.
43. ☐ Actually pick up the phone and call someone.

44. □ Have a firm handshake.
45. □ Read a magazine or visit a website on a subject you know nothing about or do not even like.
46. □ Do not burn bridges.
47. □ Read or watch something that motivates or inspires you.
48. □ Give someone a gift for no reason.
49. □ Be curious.
50. □ Keep a diary or write a blog.
51. □ Don't smoke.
52. □ Say thank you.
53. □ Believe in yourself.
54. □ Make a decision.
55. □ Spend only what you have.
56. □ Pet an animal.
57. □ Back up your files in a safe place.
58. □ Finish something you started.
59. □ Speak in front of a group.
60. □ Add at least one new entry to your network.
61. □ Do not buy crap you do not need.
62. □ Add to your emergency fund.
63. □ Sync your computer, phone, and other electronics.
64. □ Get the most from your social media accounts.
65. □ Keep your work area organized.
66. □ Do something you have neglected.

67. ☐ Do something that scares you.

68. ☐ Listen.

69. ☐ Visualize what you want.

70. ☐ Learn how to do something new.

71. ☐ Treat others the way you want to be treated.

72. ☐ Talk to a mentor.

73. ☐ Post an interesting article or blog.

74. ☐ Do not take out a loan.

75. ☐ Throw something out that you have not used in a while.

76. ☐ Dare to be different.

77. ☐ Eat a piece of chocolate.

78. ☐ Take a big breath and let it out slowly.

79. ☐ Review what is coming tomorrow before close of business today.

80. ☐ Kiss your significant other like you did the first time.

81. ☐ Climb a flight of stairs.

82. ☐ Listen to music.

83. ☐ Ignore the naysayers.

84. ☐ Smile.

85. ☐ Laugh out loud.

86. ☐ Do not give up.

87. ☐ Follow your gut feelings.

88. ☐ Look people in the eye.

89. ☐ Do not complain or speak badly of others.

90. ☐ Search your name online.

91. ☐ Spend time with family and close friends.

92. ☐ Share.

93. □ Hug someone.
94. □ Give yourself some downtime.
95. □ Read a good book.
96. □ Floss your teeth.
97. □ Wash your face before you go to bed.
98. □ Know when to quit for the day.
99. □ Relax at the end of the day with a favorite beverage and go over your day with some-one you are close to.
100. □ Turn everything off at night.
101. □ Get a good night's rest.

Good job!
Now start all over again.
Tomorrow.
And the next day.
And the next.
Every day.

Sign up for daily success tips and download
your own daily success checklist
www.daynasteele.com/rockstarsuccess

There is no point at which you can say, "Well, I'm successful now. I might as well take a nap."

—Carrie Fisher

About the Author

Dayna Steele is a serial en-
trepreneur, Hall of Fame radio
personality, media and mar-
keting strategist, the author
of *Rock to the Top: What I
Learned about Success from
the World's Greatest Rock
Stars*, and a popular business
success speaker.

Currently traveling the world,
creating rock stars with her
success presentations "Find Your Inner Rock Star,"
"I'm with the Band," and "The Rock Star Interview,"
Dayna shows individuals and companies how to grow
their business, improve performance, increase their
bottom line, and be better than the competition using
her Rock Star Principles of Success. *Reader's Digest*
calls her "One of the 35 People Who Inspire Us."

Dayna lives with her husband, author Charles Justiz, in
Seabrook, Texas. They have three sons. She is working
on her next book *I'm with the Band: Network Your Way
into Anything, Anywhere, Anytime*. Her website is www.
daynasteele.com. Follow her on Twitter @daynasteele.
Questions? Just ask: dayna@daynasteele.com.

About the Illustrator

Bill Hinds is the drawing half of the team that creates the popular, long-running sports comic strip *Tank McNamara*. He is also the creator of *Cleats* and *Sports Illustrated Kids Magazine's Buzz Beamer* comic strip. In 2001, he won the New Media Award at the National Cartoonists Society's Reuben Awards.

Hinds sold his first cartoon at age seven going door-to-door selling his crayon drawings. After his mother chastised him for bothering the neighbors, he did not try selling another cartoon until he was in college. He received his Bachelor of Fine Arts from Stephen F. Austin State University in Texas, where he was the cartoonist for the school newspaper, *The Pine Log*.

Hinds lives with his wife Lisa* and their three children in Spring, Texas. Follow him on Twitter @TankBuzzCleats.

*Lisa Waymire Hinds and Dayna Steele were best friends in elementary school. They reconnected twenty years later when Bill and Dayna appeared at the same "celebrity" charity function. There are no coincidences ... see #32.

A Final Thought

The Dalai Lama, when asked what surprised him most about humanity, answered "man," because he sacrifices his health in order to make money; then he sacrifices money to recoup his health. And then he is so anxious about the future that he does not enjoy the present, the result being that he does not live in the present or the future; he lives as if he is never going to die, and then dies having never really lived.

53450124R00096